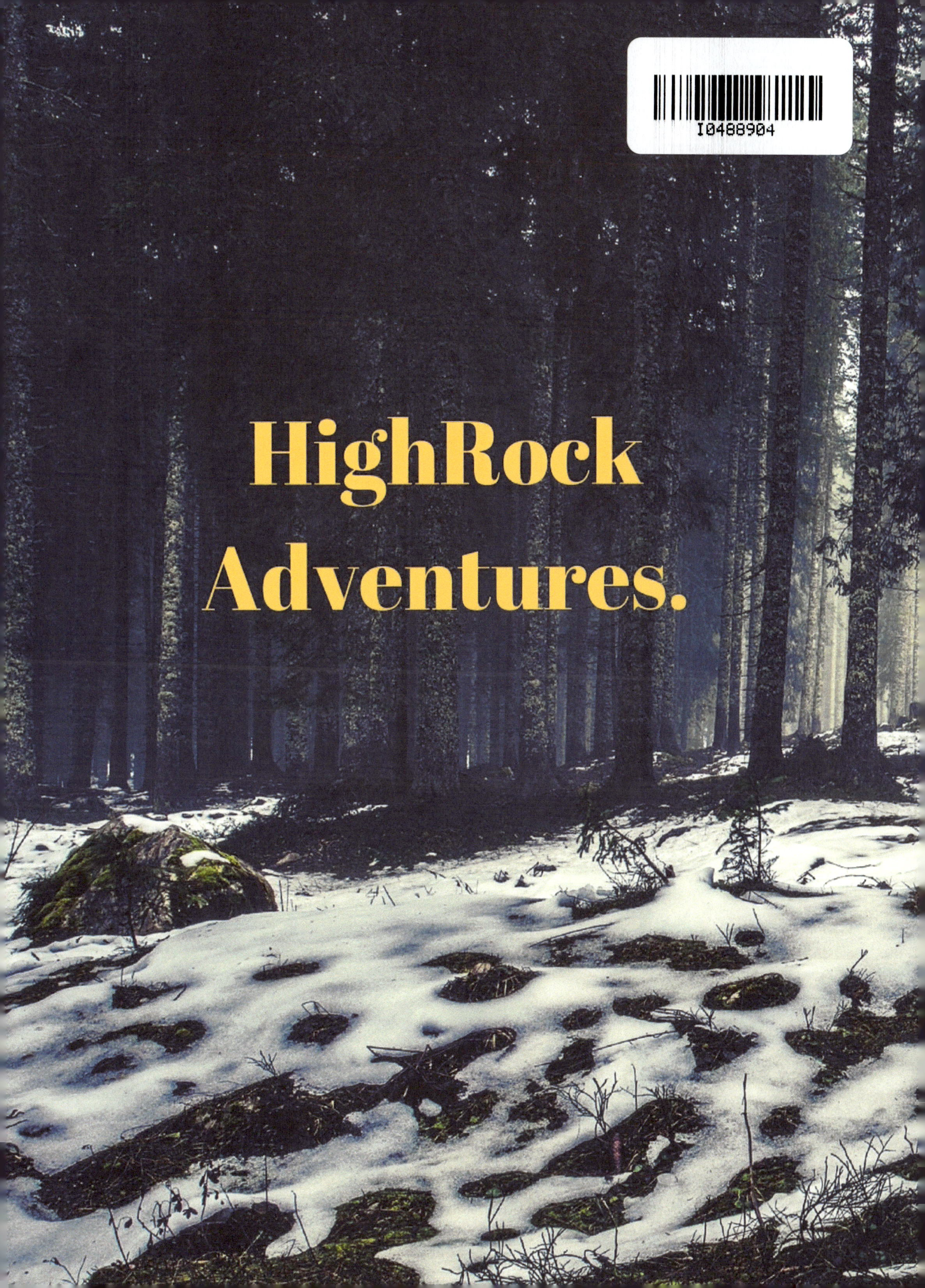

# HighRock Adventures.

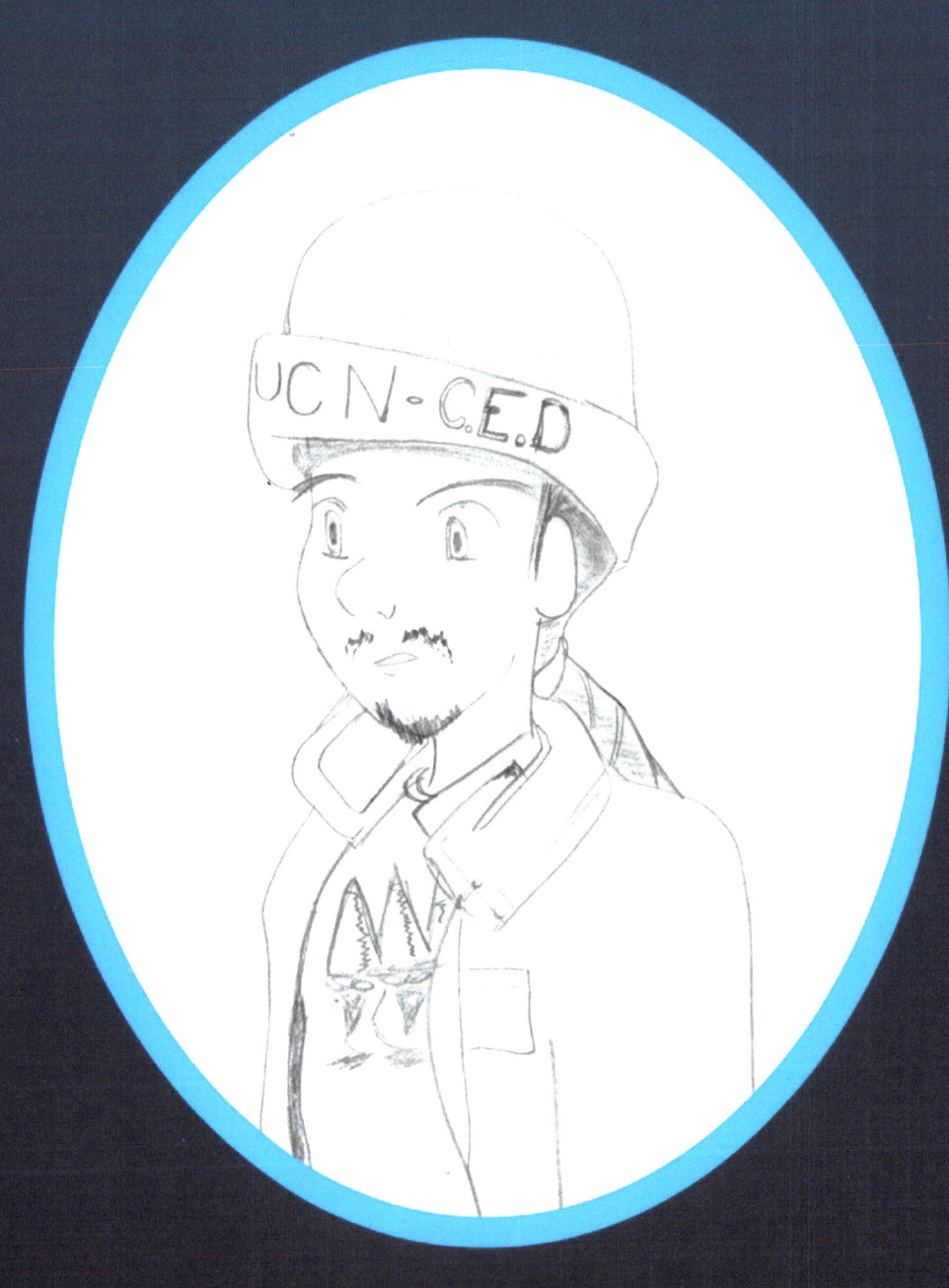

BOOK 1

HIGHROCK ADVENTURES

by Desmond Castel jr

# Acknowledgement

A BIG THANKS MRS JANICE SETO
FOR ALL THE HELP SHE PROVIDED
TO MAKE MY FIRST BOOK OF
COMICS

WOULD LIKE TO ALSO

THANK THE STUDENTS

FROM SAKASTEW SCHOOLS

GRADE 3

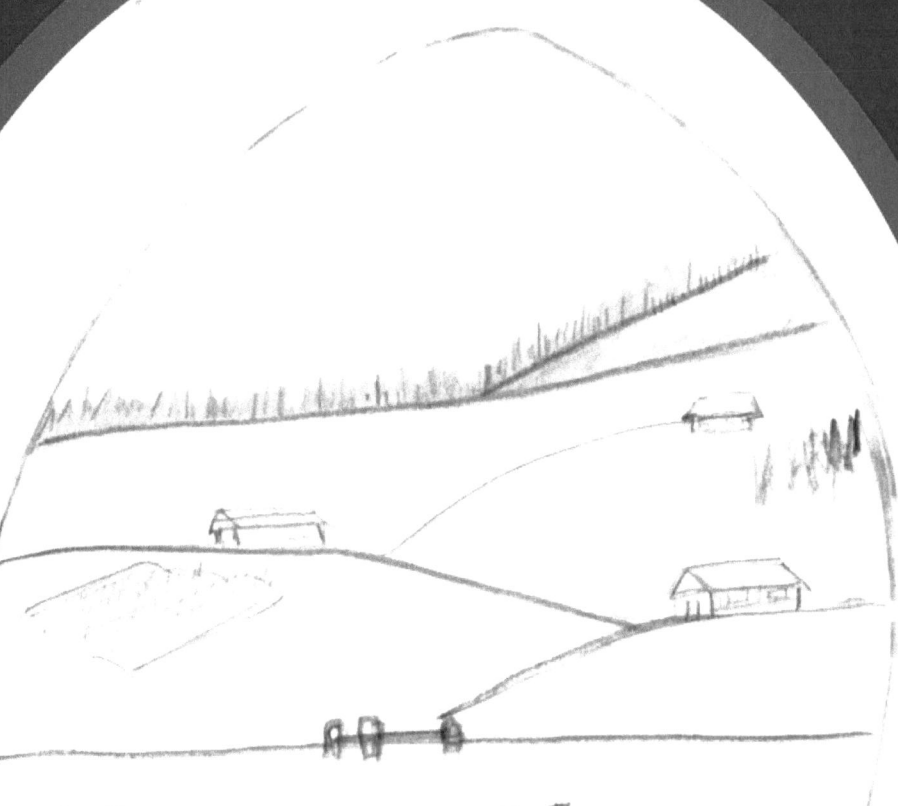

HIGH ROCK
ADVENTURES
By Daniel _____

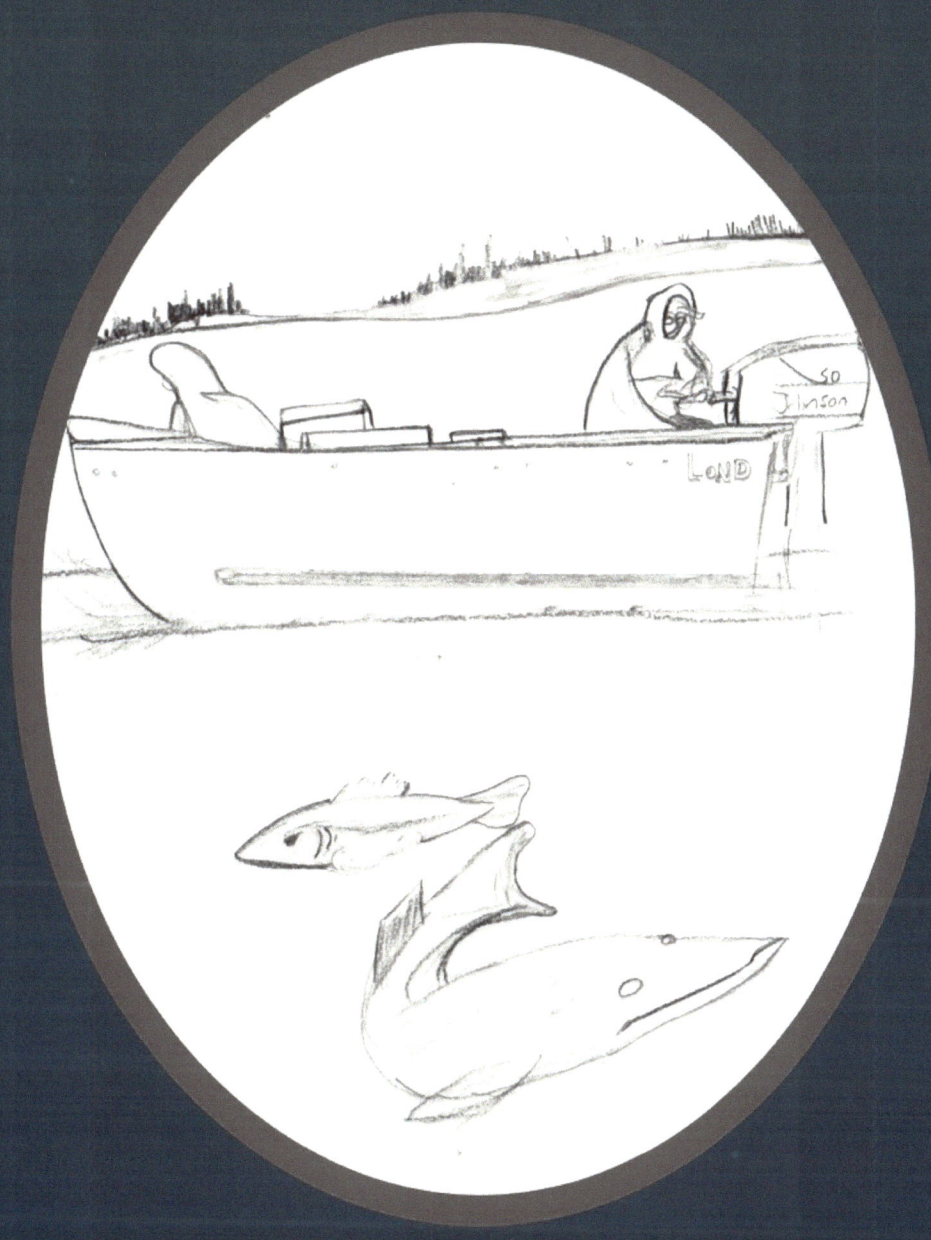

Our Story begins, As **Hunter** and **Lee** are making their way home with cargo and grocery's from Pukatawagan's Northren Store

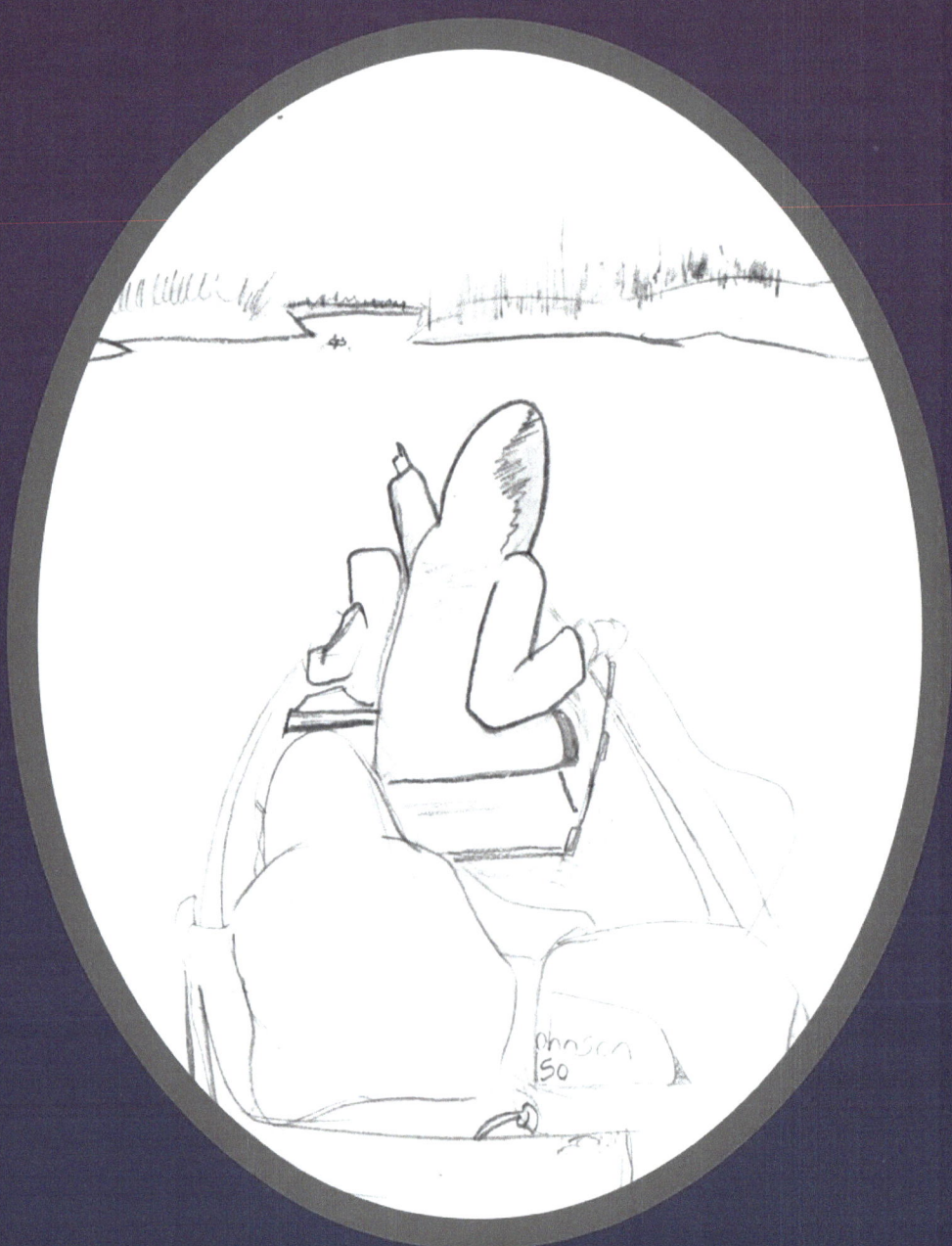

Seeing Hunter and Lee approach the entrance of Highrock, the people are excited to get their letters and news along with fresh supplies, but can't leave till they pull up there fishing nets.

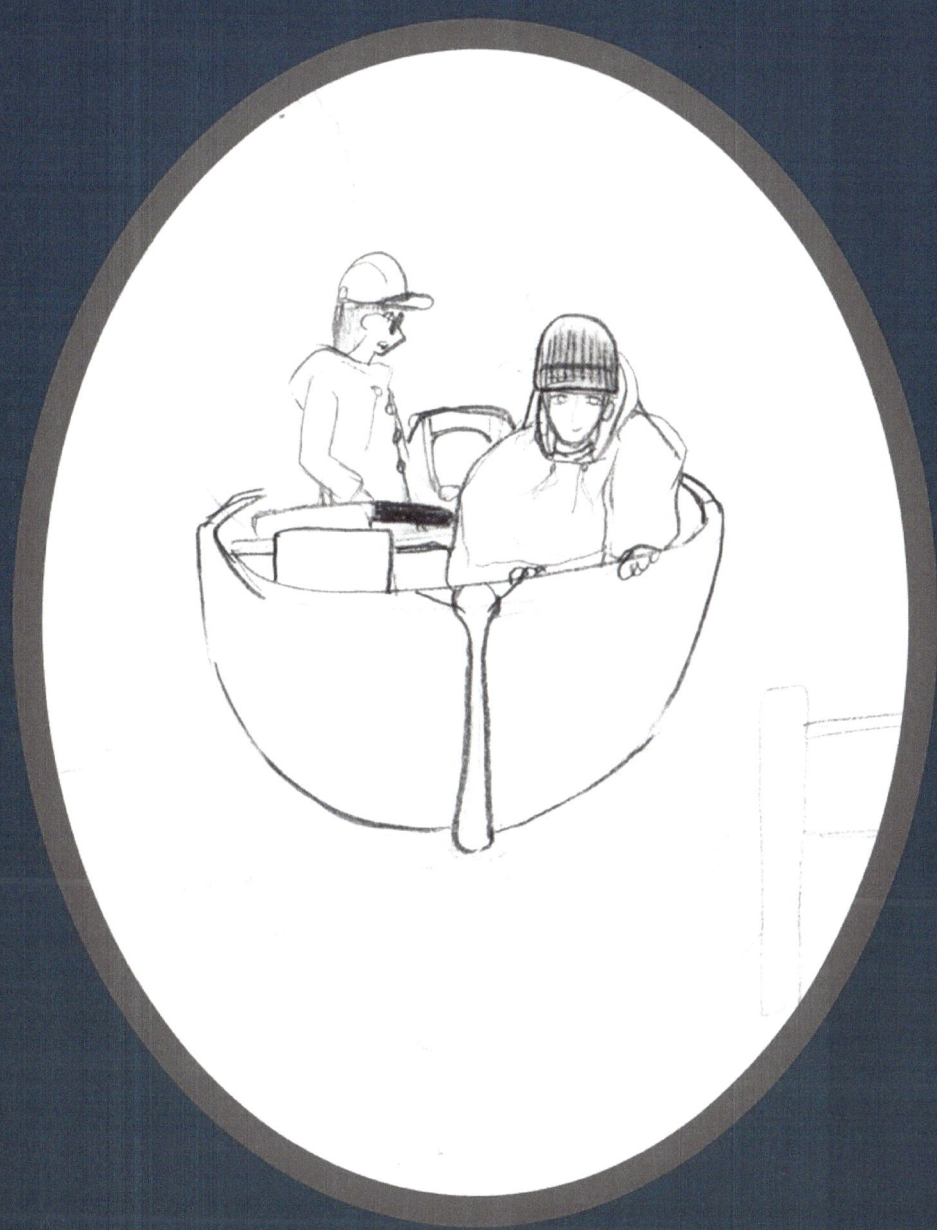

Lee calls out to Hunter, "get ready to catch the boat before it hits the dock"
Seeing that they finally made the long trip home he is ready to dock.

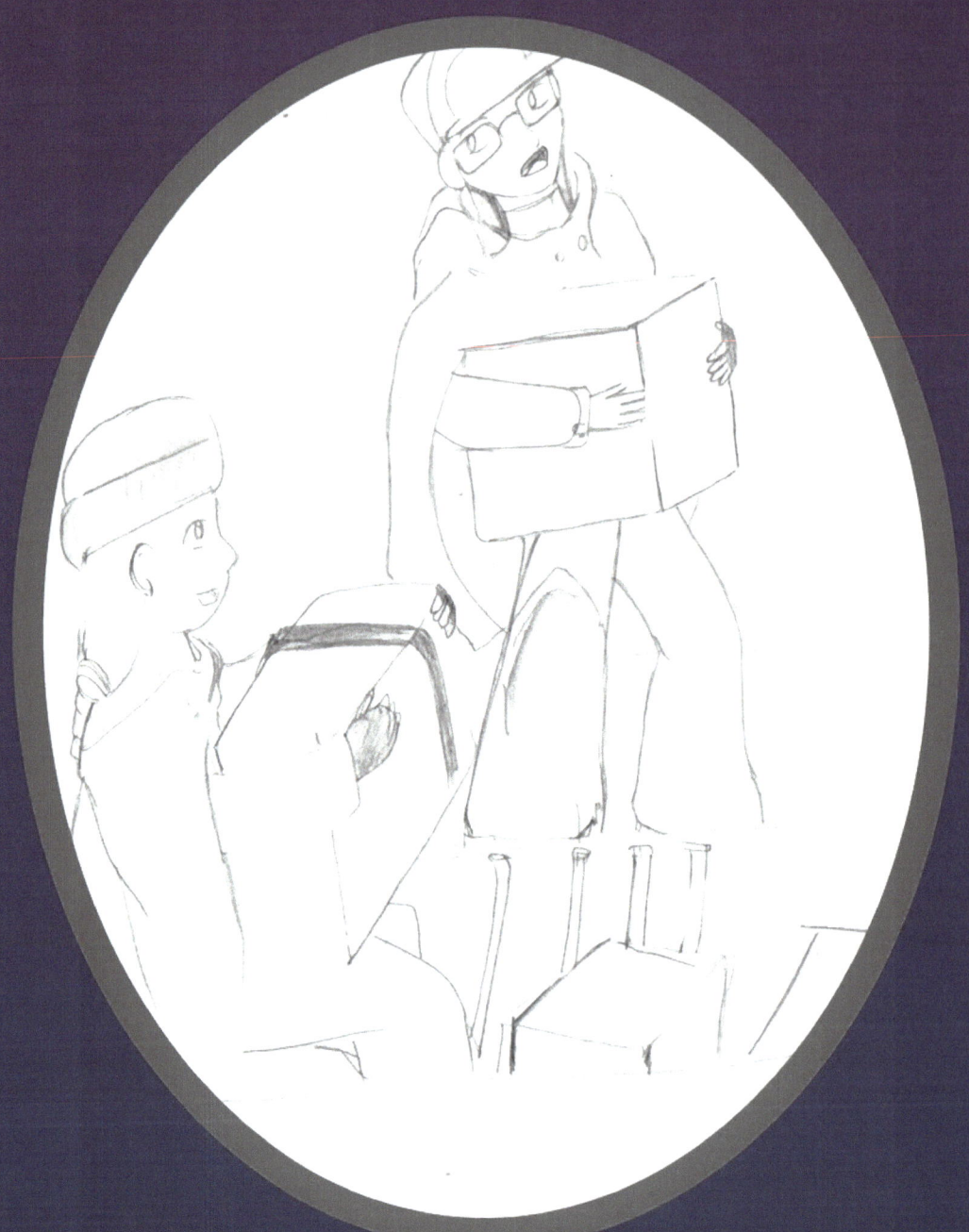

Hunter "Hey Lee are you sure Grandpa let you use his favorite hat?"

Lee " don't worry im sure he has his other favorite hat on besides we were in a rush to get to pukatwagan im sure he would understand."

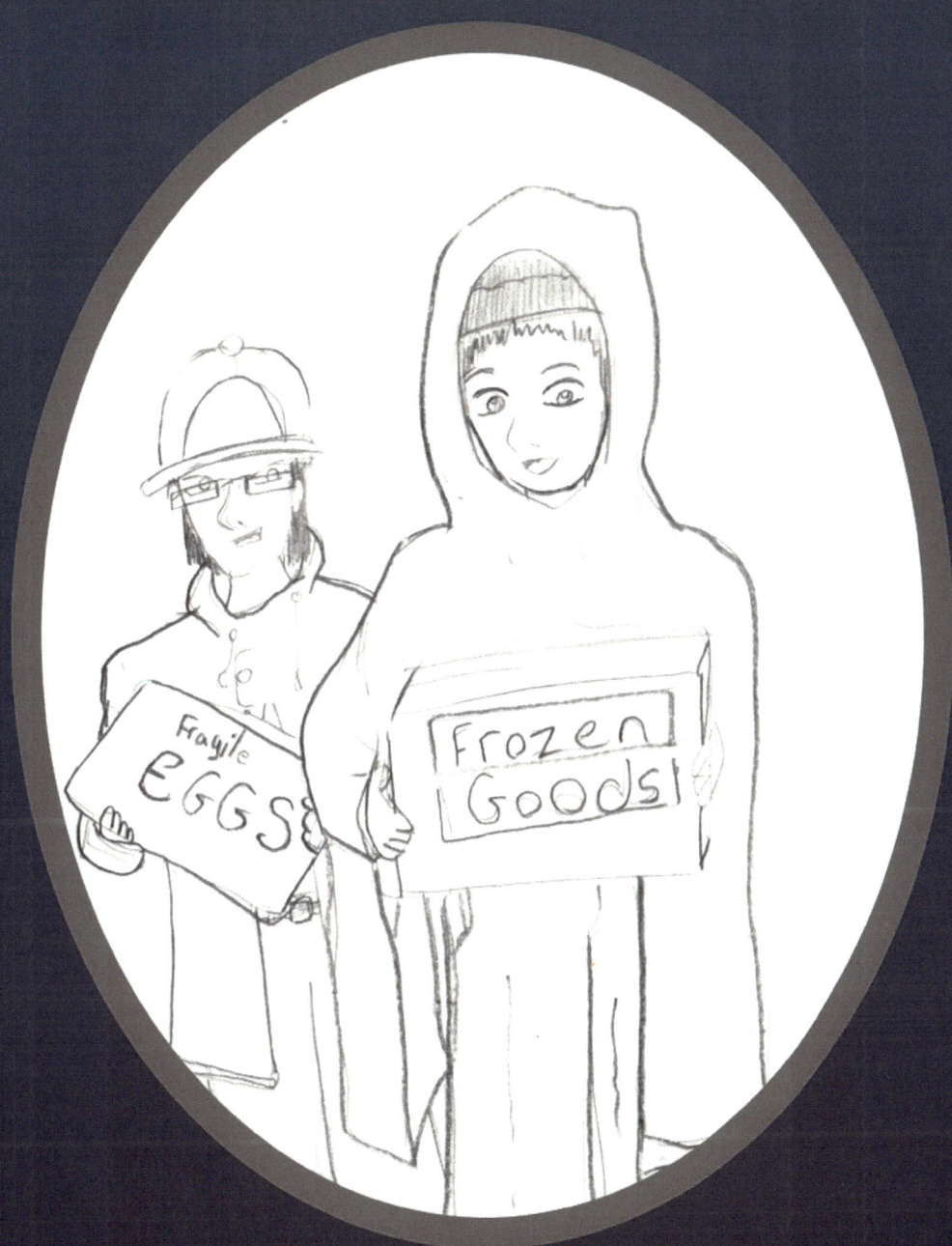

Hunter " I don't think you learned your
lesson the first time you took his hat.
Lee " hahahaha field work was the worst,
but im sure he wouldn't do that again.

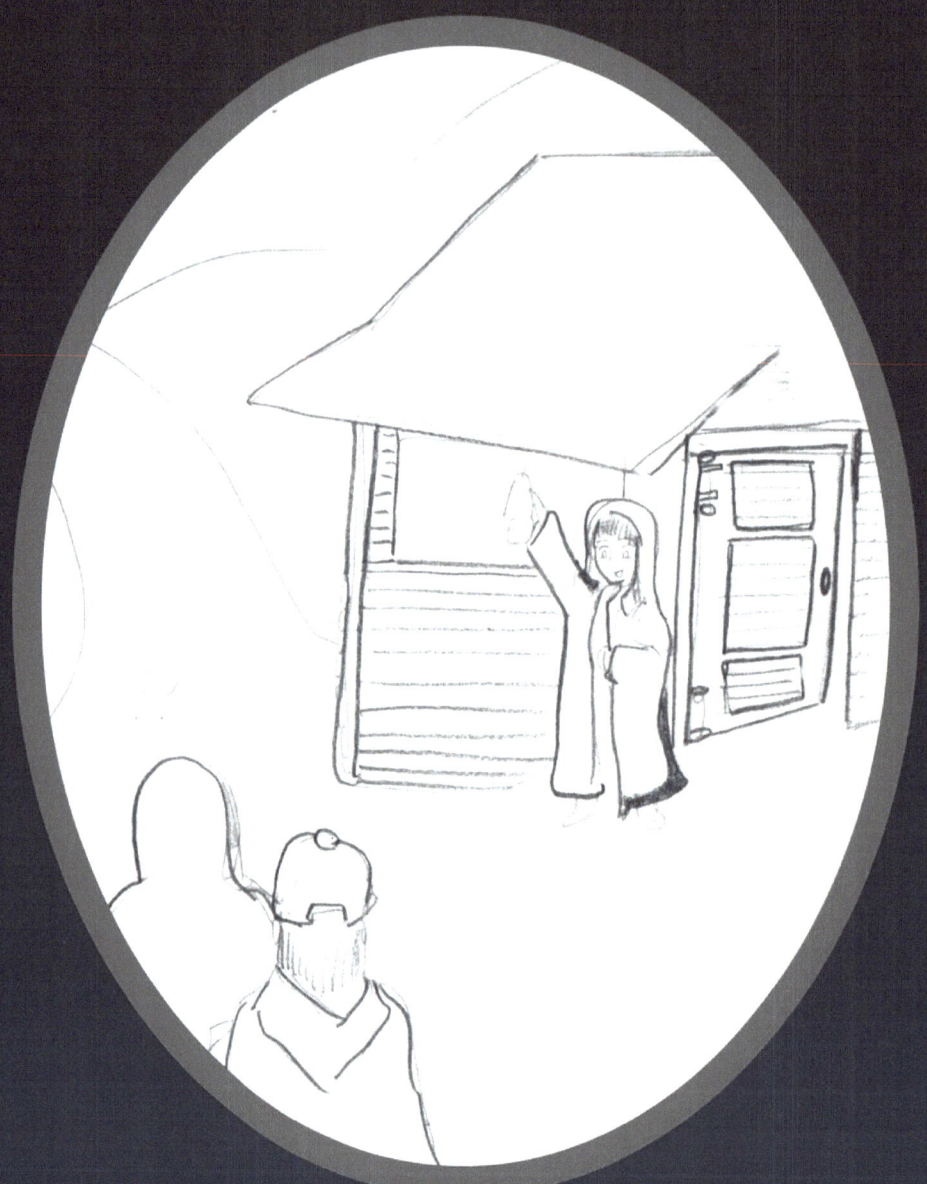

Aunt Kristina " Hey Hunter! Lee! come over here for a while, need to tell you something."
Hunter " Sure aunty what can we help you with? "

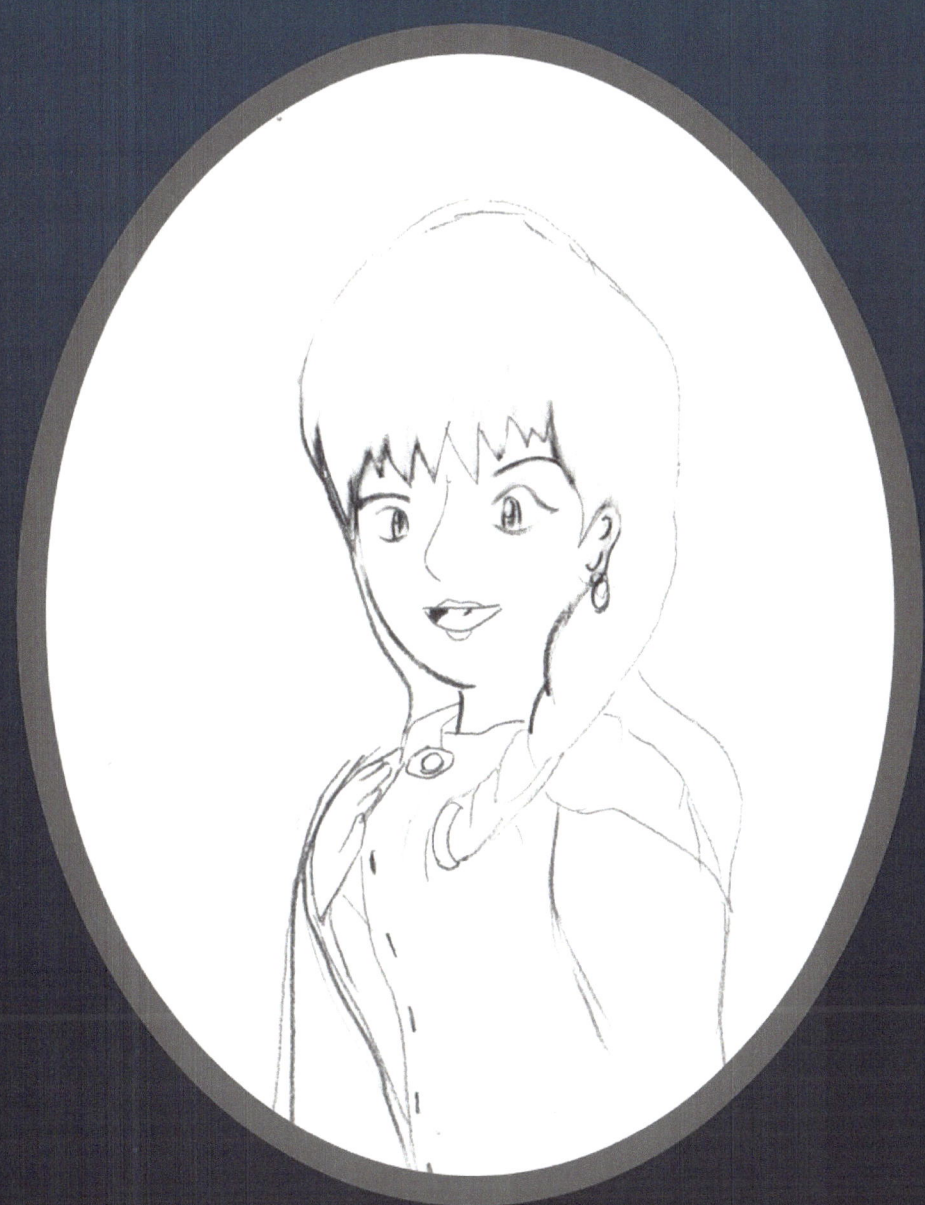

Aunt Kristina " so it is true you do have grandpa's hat on Lee, which reminds me Hunter, Grandma asked if you are still going to take them to Blueberry Hill this afternoon?

Hunter " as soon as we drop off our stuff ready to go.

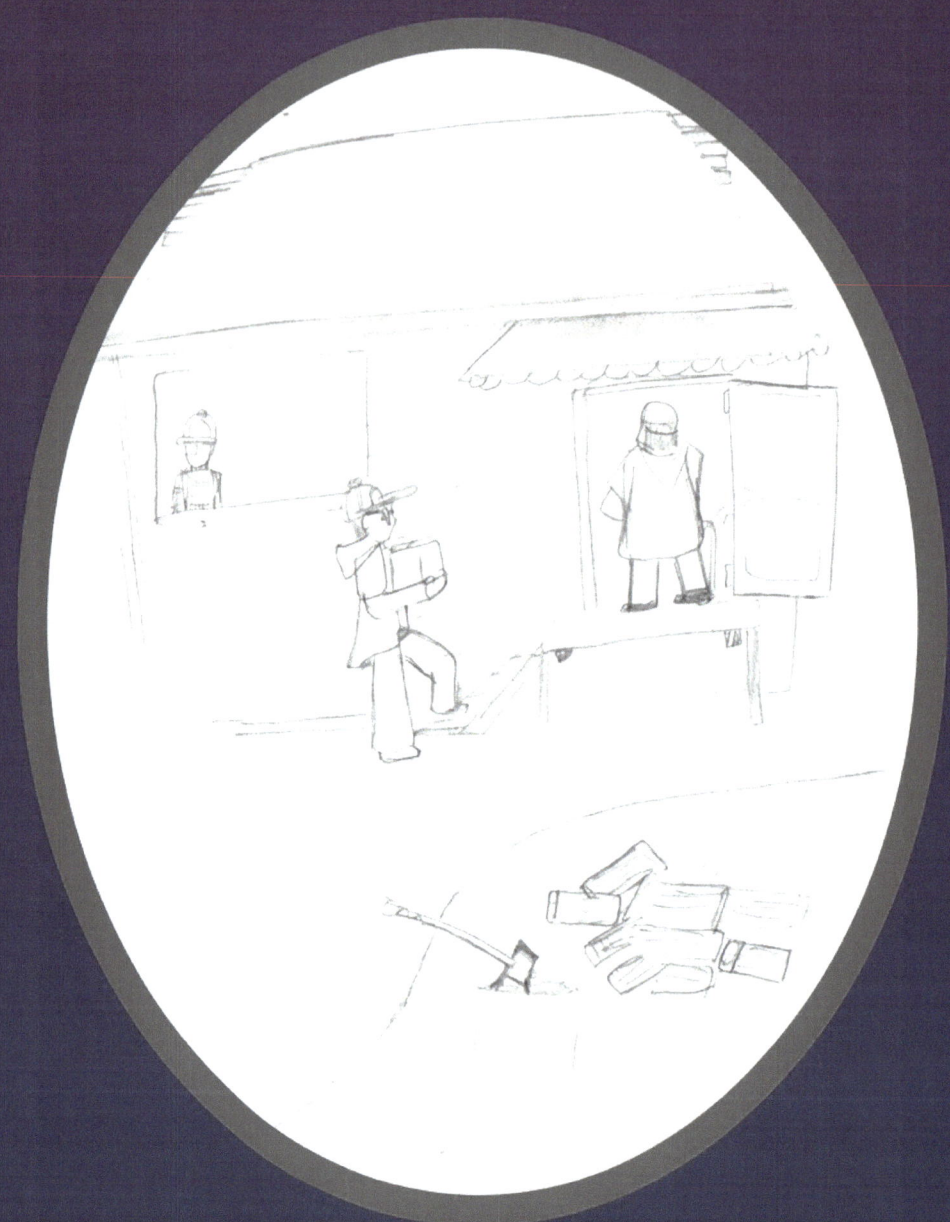

Hunter " Grandpa, Grandma we are home, and we got all the items you needed grandma, and when ever your ready we can go to Blueberry hill.
Grandpa and Grandma "Welcome home boy's.

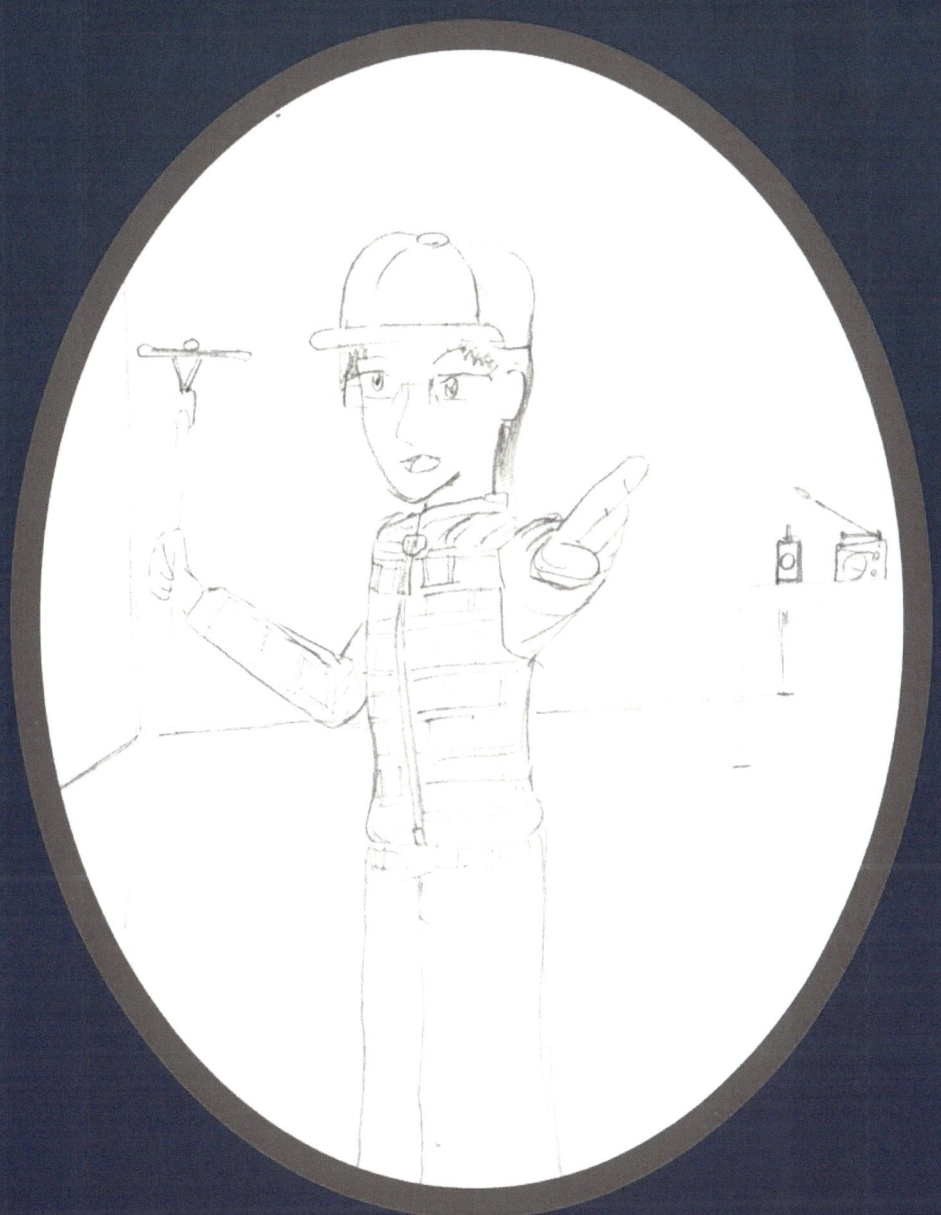

Grandpa " Lee! if your going to wear my hat you are going to do the work that comes with that hat, Grandpa grabs the garden tool and points "

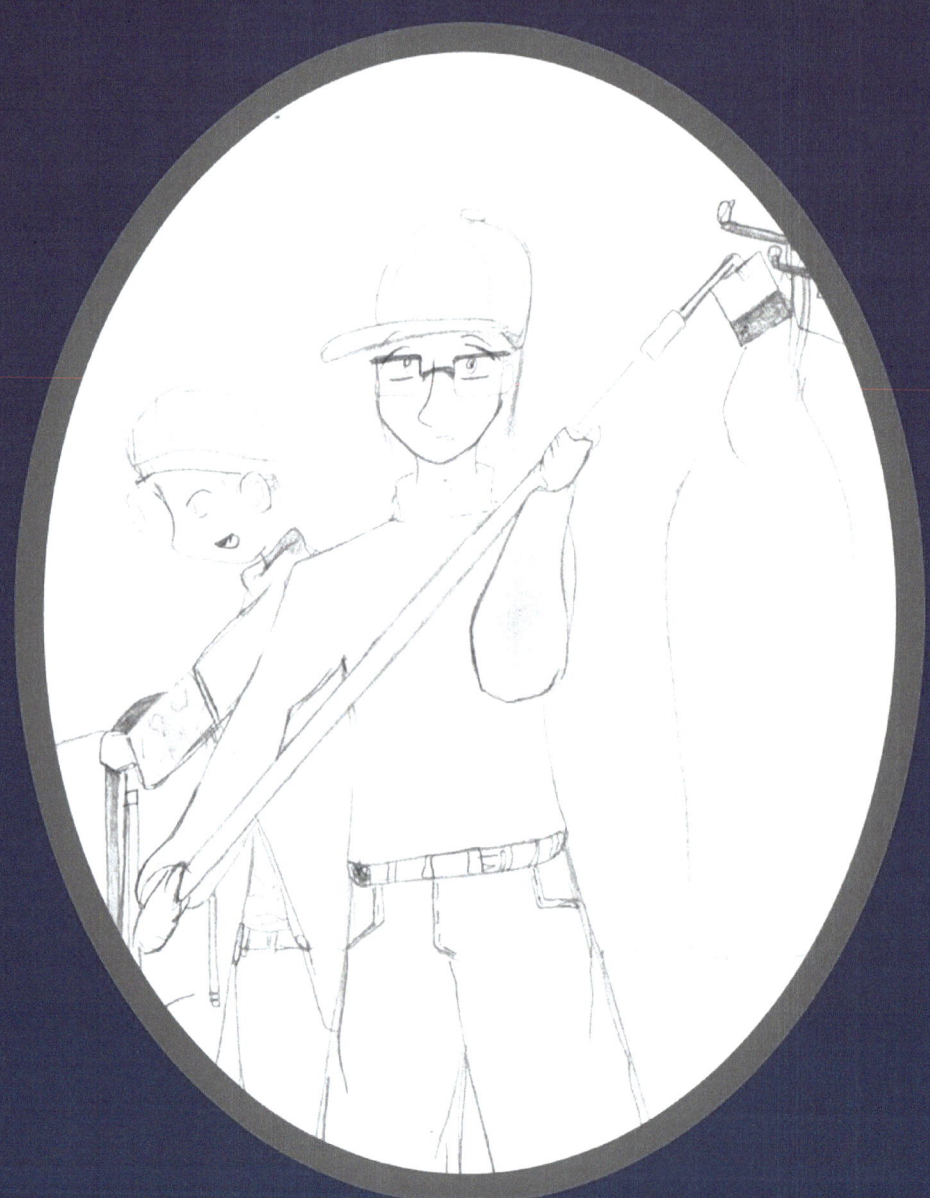

Hunter " I'll get my gear ready."
Grandpa gives the garden tool to Lee,
"get to work Lee i expect to have potatoes
with the fish supper we are going to be
having tonight.

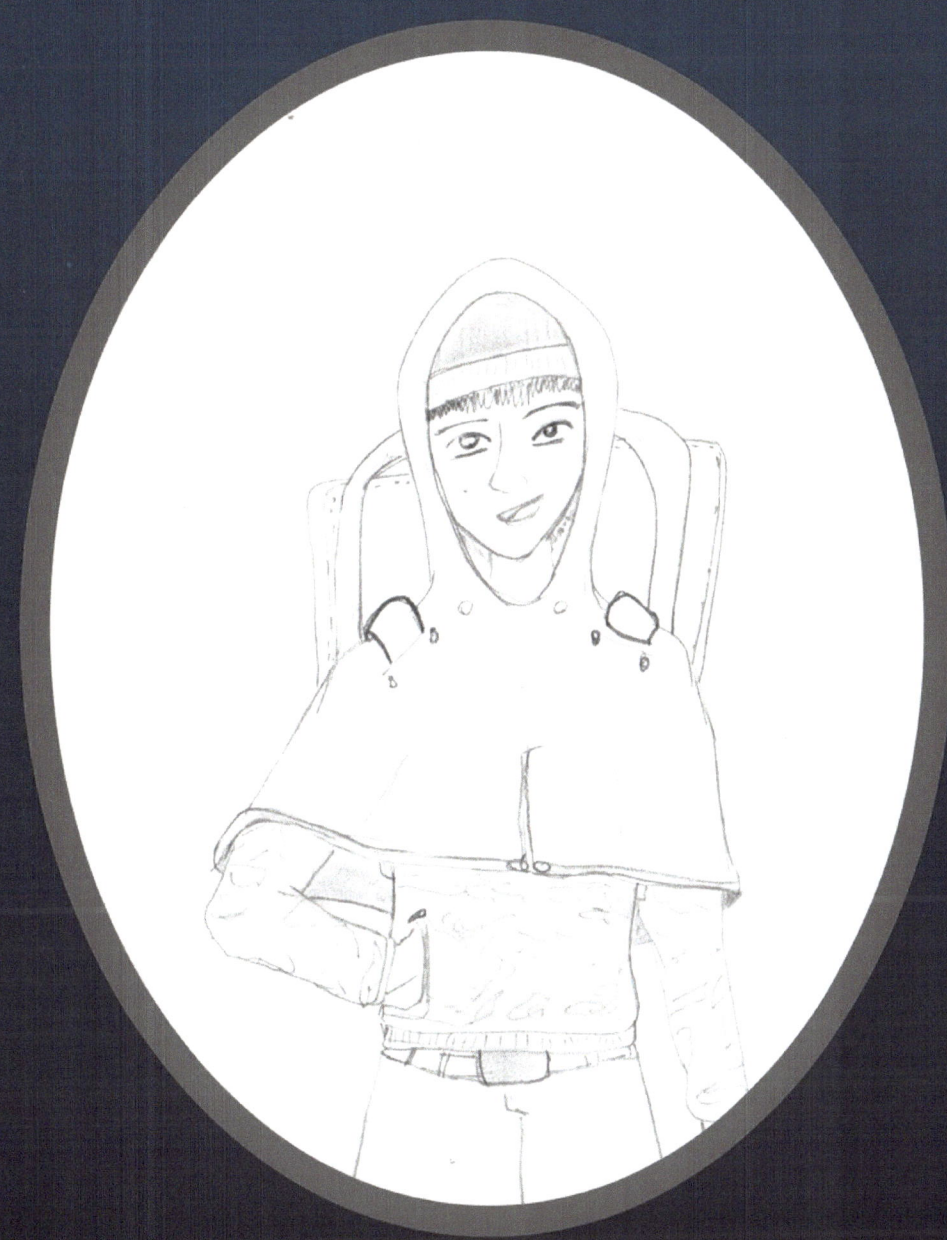

Hunter " Ready to go Grandpa and
Grandma, you guys ready to get going?

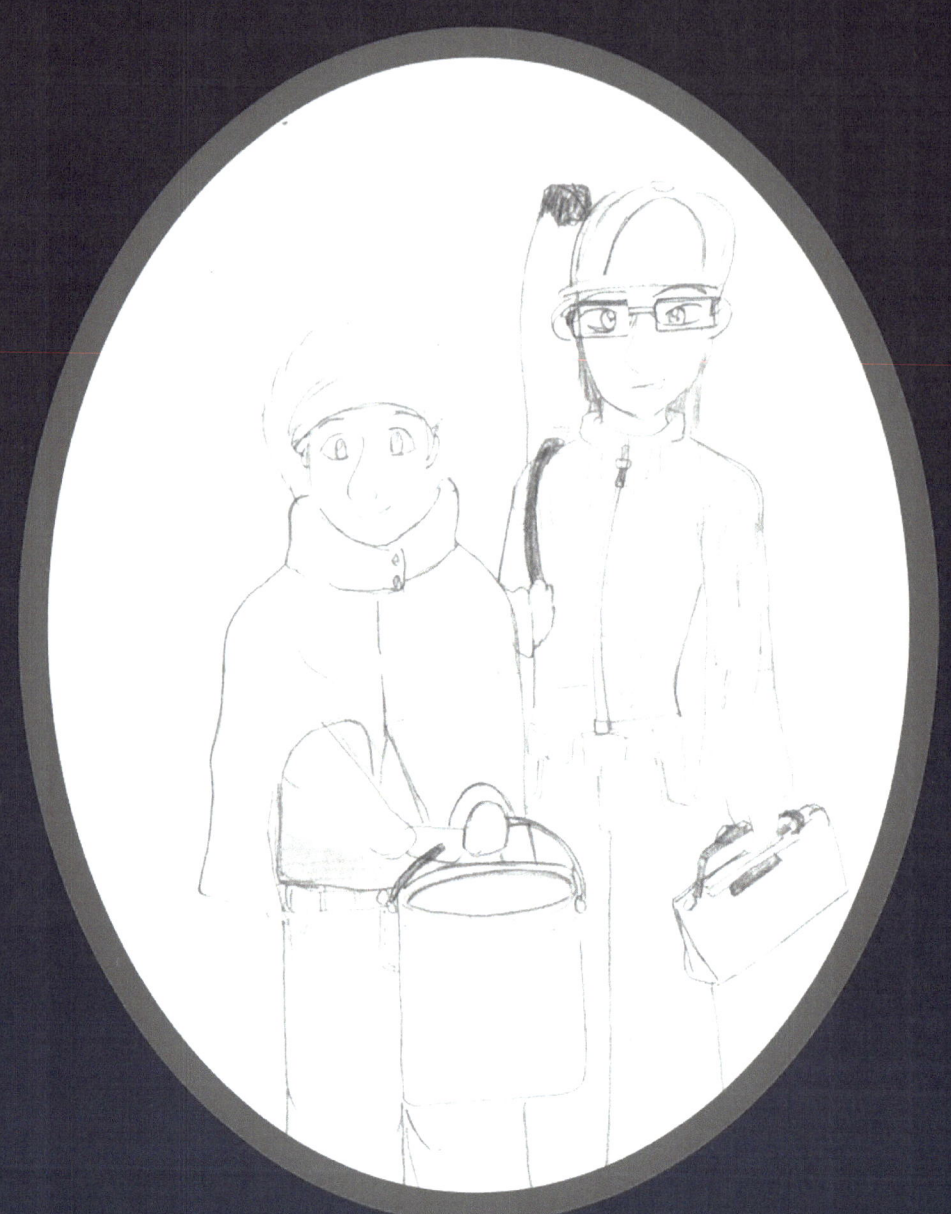

Grandpa and Grandma are planning
 " We are ready to go Hunter, you do
know the way right? "
 " Don't forget to bring the extra
buckets and did you pack our
snacks? "

As Hunter and his grandparents begin to make their way to the boat, they wave good bye to lee who's tending to the garden found near the cabin.

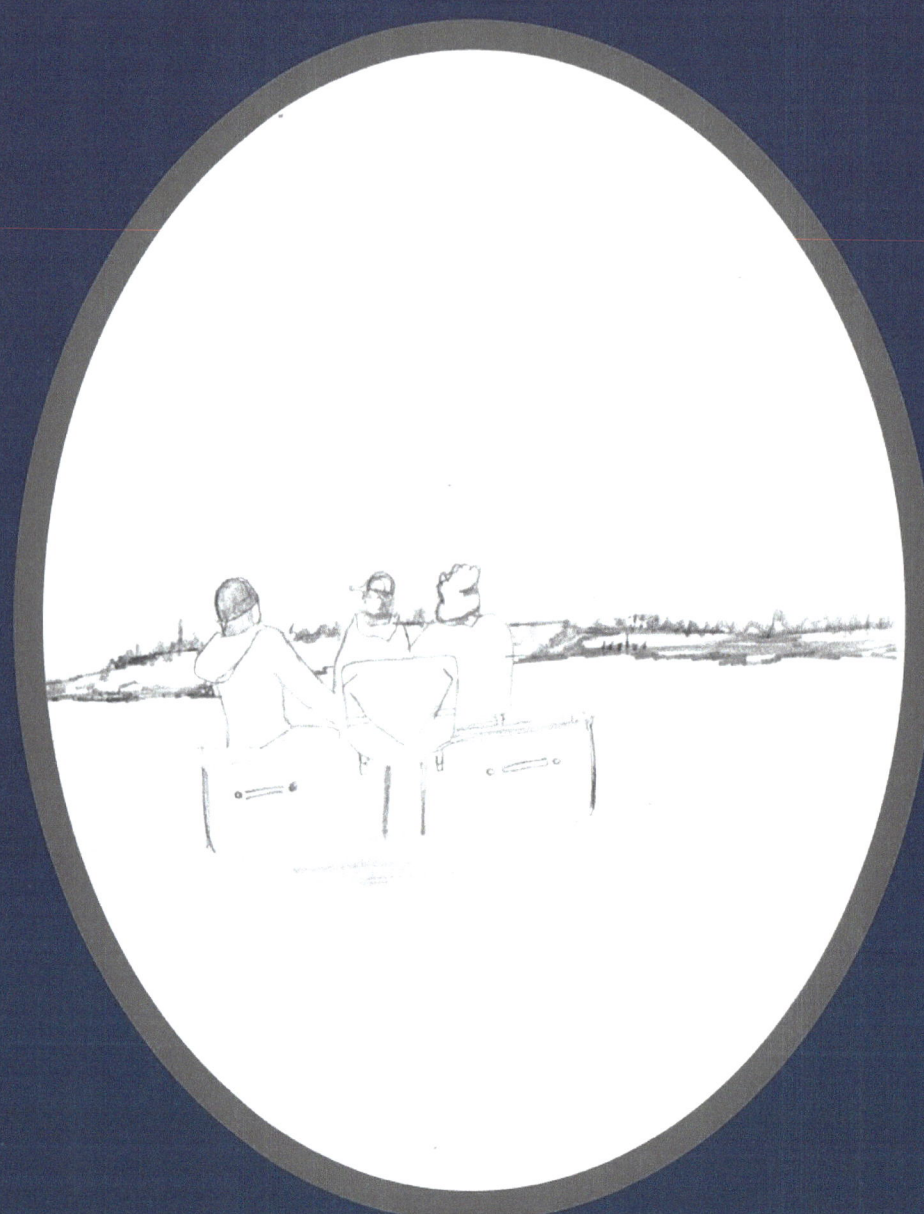

Enjoying the ride to blueberry hill grandpa tells a story about the first time they went to blueberry hill and how much berries they picked.

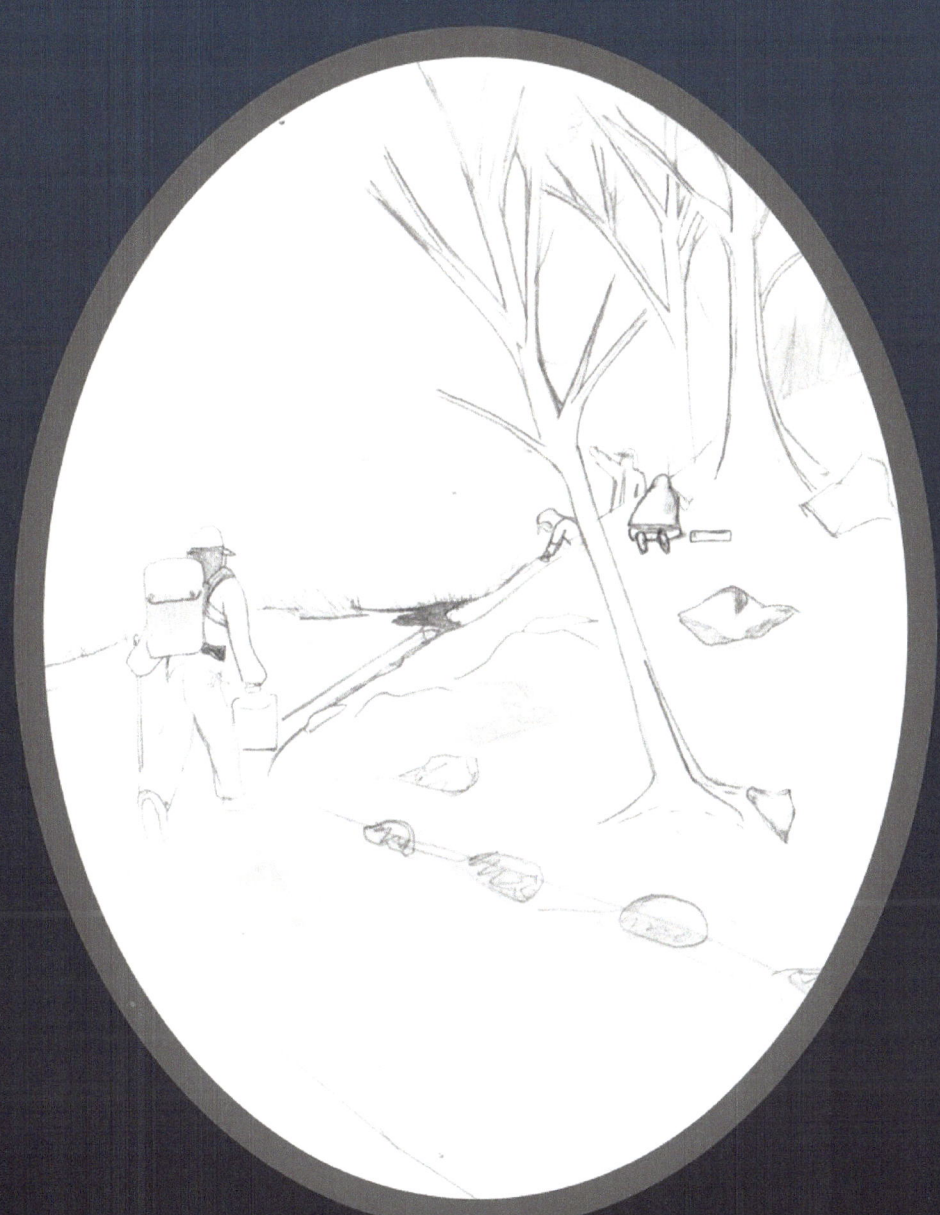

Upon arriving they seen other boats near the dock, knowing that others are already on the hill picking berrys they rushed over to find a spot to pick berry's.

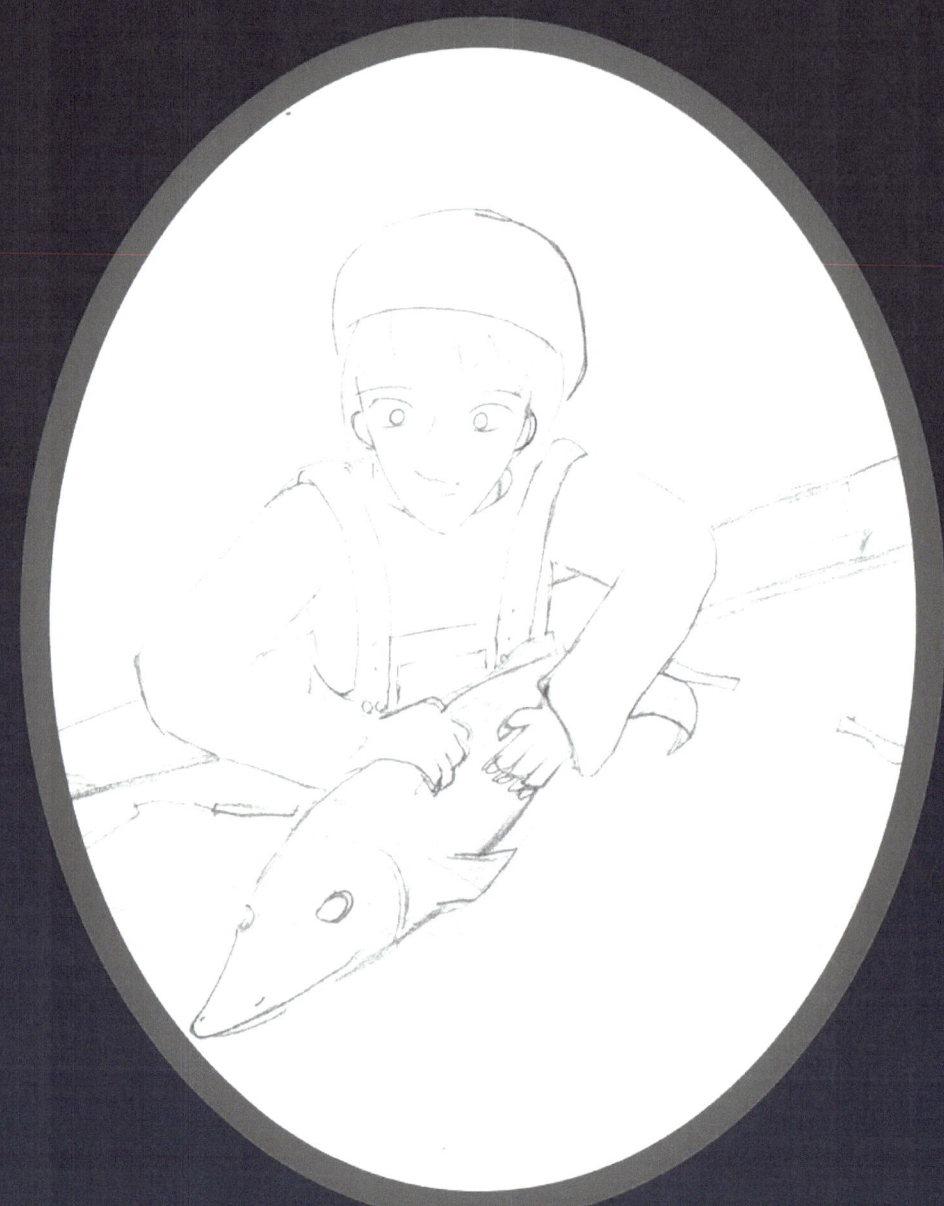

While Grandpa and Grandma went to pick berries they asked hunter to go check the nets to see if they are going to be having fish for supper, feeling lucky he caught a northern pike.

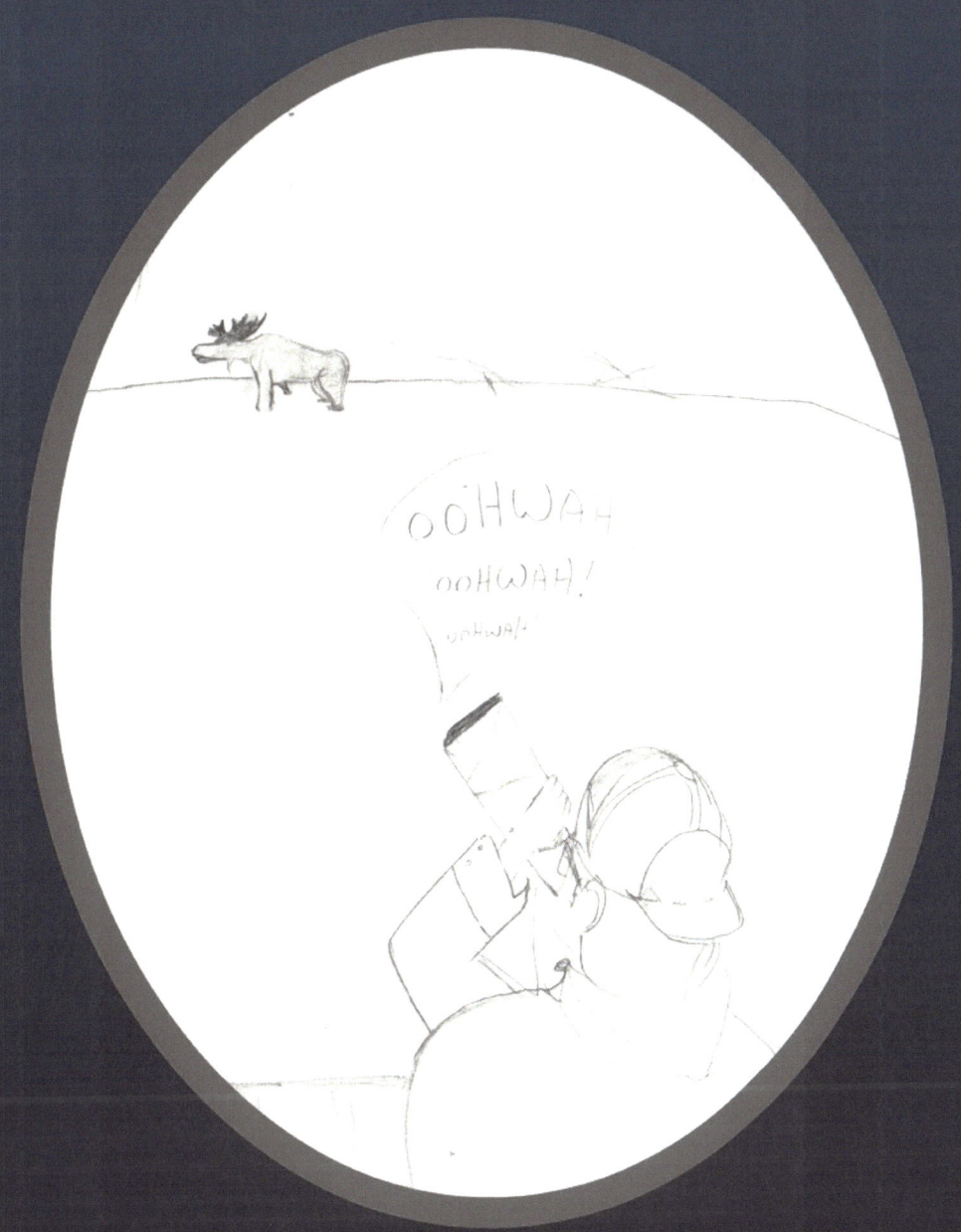

And to his Surprise he sees a Bull moose grazing across from where he was pulling up his net, he then pulls out a moose caller and started to call out to the bull moose.

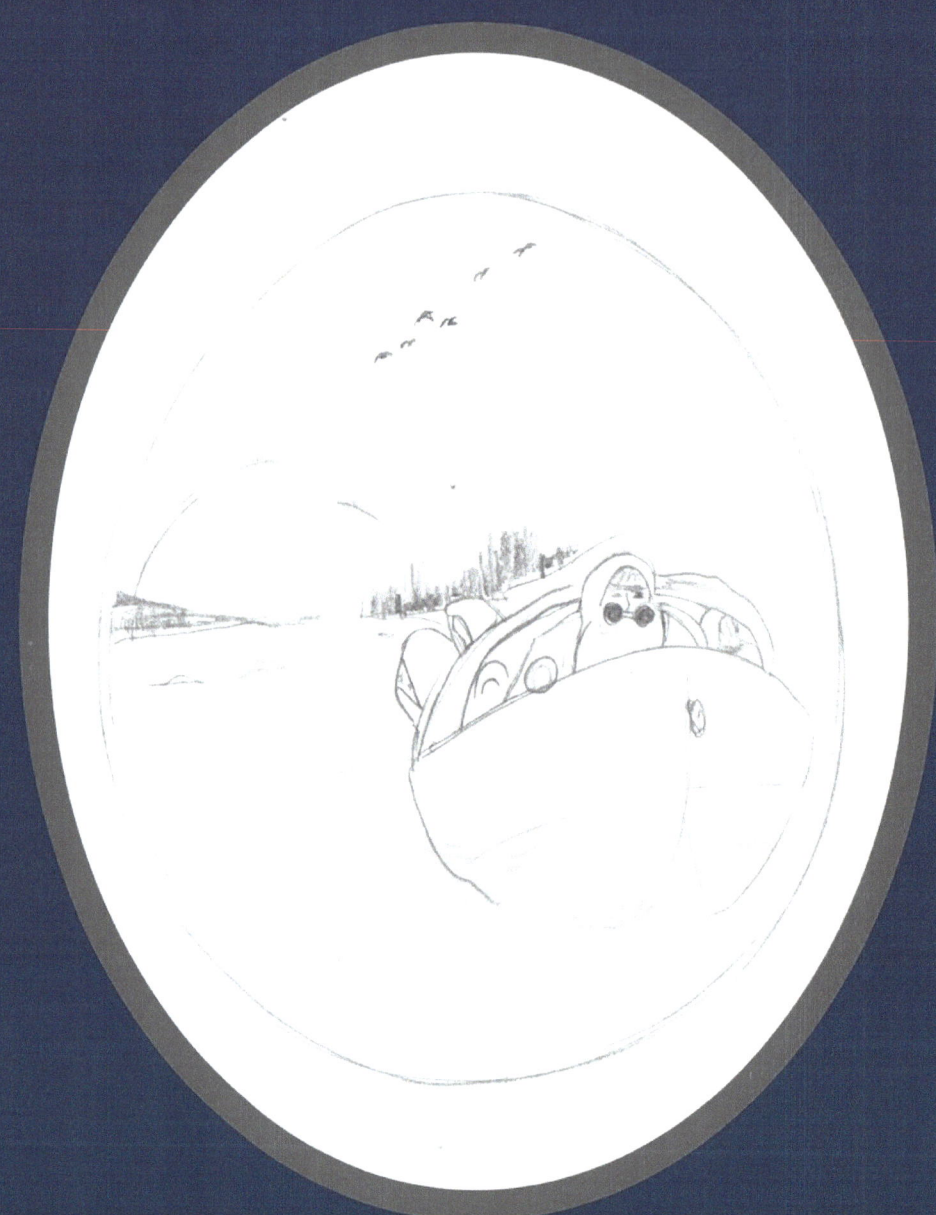

But tomorrow is another day of Adventures and Stories.
Till next time To Be Continued.

# EXTRA Content.

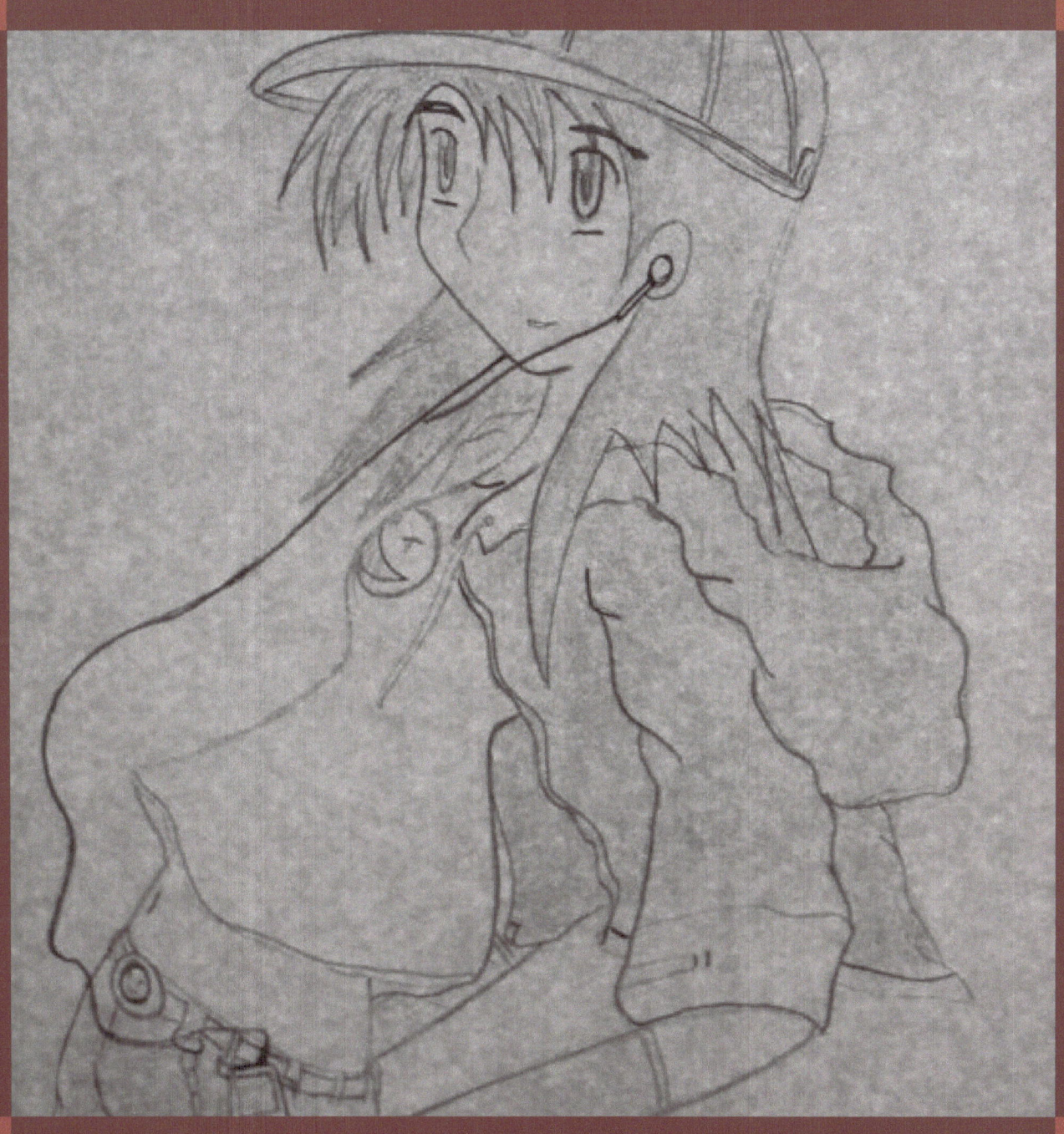

# EXTRA Content.

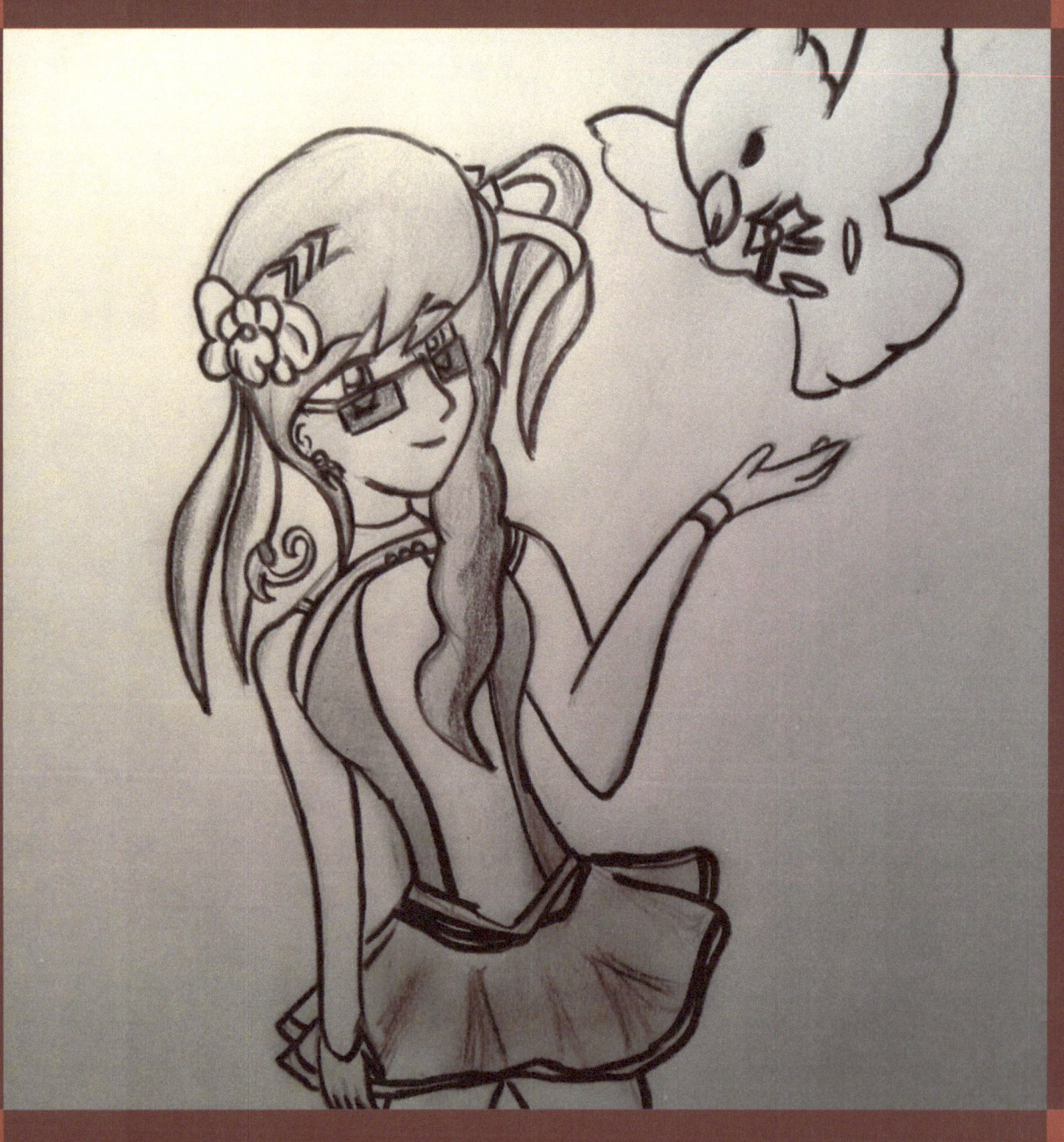

# EXTRA Content.

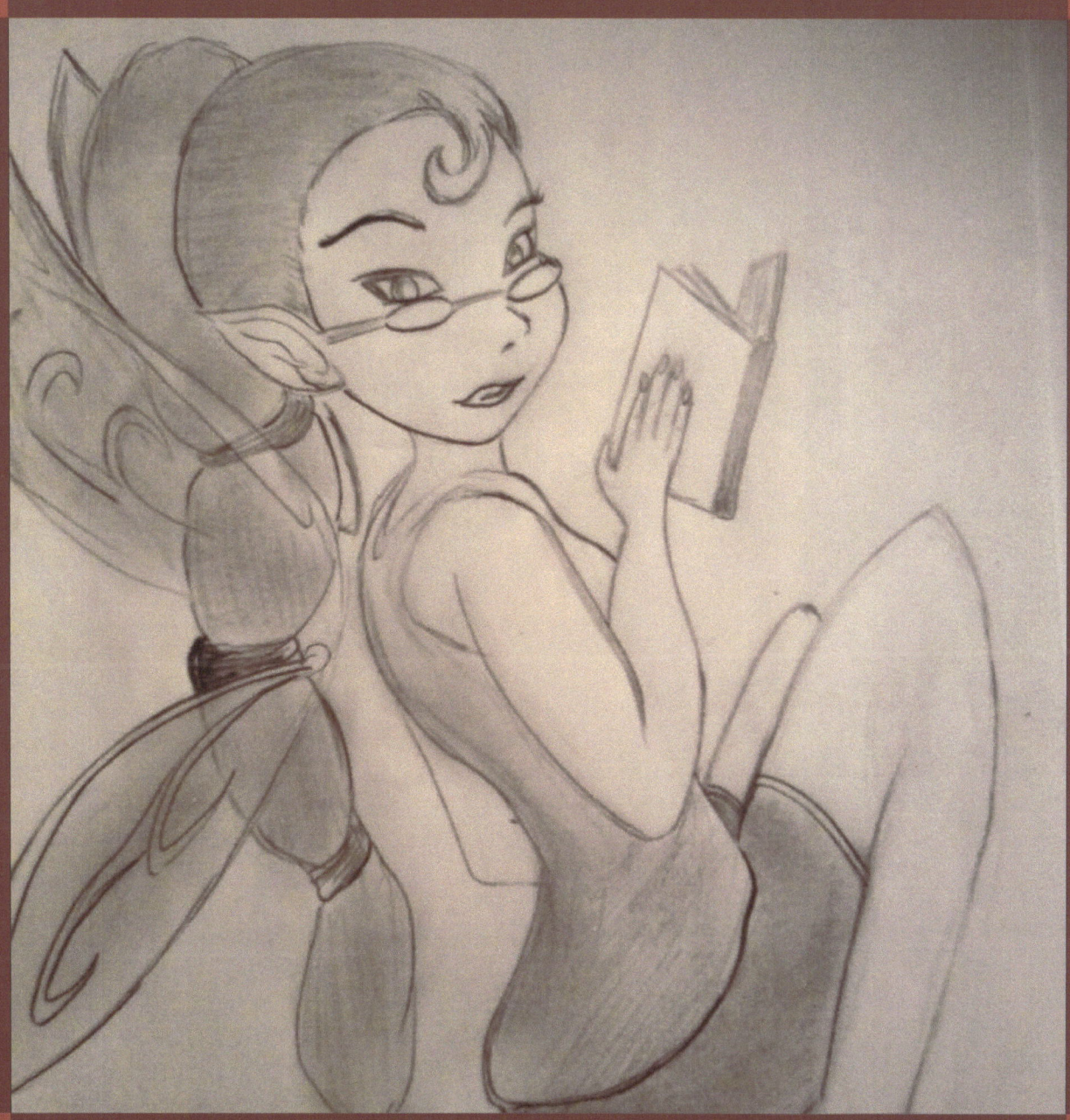

Highrock Adventures
Book 1 of Cree Adventures
series

Copyright 2017 by Desmond
Castel Jr

ISBN: 978-0-9958404-0-9
(print)
ISBN: 978-0-9958404-1-6
(ebook)

www.ingramcontent.com/pod-product-compliance
Lightning Source LLC
Chambersburg PA
CBHW050911180526
45159CB00007B/2878